Lowland

Julie,

Some fictional bits here and there (e.g. p. 43 & 63), but otherwise all true... For best results, read this in one sitting (c. 1 hour); if you're not clear on a poem, just move on to the next one! Much here for any Psychology student - or teacher!

With thanks and best wishes, Will

15.5.18.

WILL KEMP

INDEPENDENT INNOVATIVE INTERNATIONAL

Published by Cinnamon Press
Meirion House,
Glan yr afon,
Tanygrisiau
Blaenau Ffestiniog,
Gwynedd,
LL41 3SU
www.cinnamonpress.com

ISBN: 978-1-907090-94-3

British Library Cataloguing in Publication Data. A CIP record for this book can be obtained from the British Library.

Designed and typeset in Palatino by Cinnamon Press
Cover from original artwork 'Reflection of Reeds in Water' by Rudolph Robertze © Rudolph Robertze; agency: dreamstime.com
Cover design by Cottia Fortune-Wood & Jacob Hull

Printed in Poland

Cinnamon Press is represented in the UK by Inpress Ltd www.inpressbooks.co.uk and in Wales by the Welsh Books Council www.cllc.org.uk

Acknowledgements

Thanks to the editors of journals in which these and other poems have appeared: *Acumen, Aesthetica, Ambit, Cake, Dawntreader, Envoi, Equinox, Essence, Fourteen, The French Literary Review, The Guardian, Haiku Quarterly, The Interpreter's House, Iota, The Journal, Magma, The New Writer, The North, Obsessed with Pipework, Orbis, Other Poetry, Poetry Cornwall, Poetry News, Poetry Scotland, The SHOp, Smith's Knoll.*

Thanks too to Carole Bromley, Carol-Ann Duffy, Doreen Gurrey, Ann and Peter Sansom, Susan Richardson, Robert Minhinnick, Helen Cadbury, Ged, Jackie, Dave, Jan and everyone at Cinnamon.

And a special thanks to Sibylle, for providing the higher ground.

About the author

Will Kemp studied at Cambridge and UEA before working as an environmental planner in Canada, Holland and New Zealand. In 2010 he won the Envoi International Poetry Prize and the Cinnamon Press Poetry Collection Award. His first collection, *Nocturnes*, was published by Cinnamon in 2011. *Lowland* is his second collection. His third collection, *The Painters Who Studied Clouds*, will be published in 2015.

Contents

I. Fenland

II. Holland

III. Waterland

Notes   80

*To
my family and friends,
for standing by me*

Lowland

I. Fenland

Holland

It starts with a spit jutting into the tide
to form a strand that won't wash away,
the land little more than sea, a place for
seafarers to stop, wrecked, find at least
they can fish from this spot, or vanish
into the mist by the shore; but by now
it's the seventeenth century, and that
clump of shacks has become a village,
harbour, port – with fields drained
by polders, dykes, windmills – and
that port is a city, and that city rules
the world, and its ships are returning
from the Orient and Dutch East Indies
laden with china, spices and pearls,
and its painters are doing lobsters,
lemons and carpets; and a girl stands
by a window pouring milk into a bowl.

Holland Fen

Another September,
flat land caught

in the long amber
of late afternoon:

reeds, drains etched
into waves of fields,

that poplar a spire
on the horizon,

where a plane lays
a vapour trail

as if to underline
the dominance of sky.

Kesteven

Slung across
the blue glow of sun-drained light

a stave of telephone wires
pegged with starlings

which now burst
to pepper the sky in flight

Lincolnshire

I scramble up the bank past
Liz to become king of the castle
with that moat of slow, dirty water.
You'll not find it so funny if we have to
paddle home, Nan grins in pink wellies
and fifties specs, before reminding us
of Peter and the Dyke then mapping out
the corners of our kingdom – Caistor,
New Holland, Goole, Gainsborough;
a pancake of cornfields stetching
all the way from the blue Wolds
to Dutch River. And at once
I roley-poley down the slope
to find a spring to stick my finger in
and save the whole wide world.

Nine

The lawn was always ready for a Cup Final,
the woods by the road a lost kingdom waiting
to be discovered. I rode my bike standing up,

taking off from ramps of roots, walked home
from school practising leg-spin or duelling
with the Cardinal's men at every tree.

Happiness was reading Asterix on my bed
with a bar of chocolate without Jane playing
My Sweet Lord again and again in her room.

Wanted a model of a Messerschmidt 109E
(with desert camouflage) for Christmas,
and a sword like Lancelot's to fight off

2B at the school gates when I rescued
Denise Thompson from a burning stake
because she looked like Truly Scrumptious.

I was *not* going to grow into Liz's flares
or do her belly-dance with the hula hoop
Auntie Molly brought back from Hawaii,

but *was going to* eat my mother's stollenbrot,
catch her smoking while doing the ironing,
ask why streams were never blue.

Went to bed thinking of snow and fireworks,
the banana and sugar sandwiches we ate
on the lawn with lemon squash in summer;

and knelt to say The Lord's Prayer out loud
every night – eyes shut, hands together –
to make sure she didn't die.

Dutch River

Liz kept score of who fell in –
Jake the beagle five times,
me a close-run four –
though best of all was
her one and only plunge:
that quiet plop
as our parents bickered
about some lock,
then her best breast-stroke
through the brown –
head craned high,
not once glancing
at the banks of anglers
who one by one raised
their lines as if saluting
the passing Queen.

Cruyff

The World Cup finals, 1974:
diving headers, long-range shots,
swapping stickers in the playground.

And everyone doing *that* turn:
the feint left but the ball heeled right,
then the swivel and stride past
the O-mouthed defender, with time

to look up – elbows shoulder-high
as if treading water or conducting
an orchestra – and stroke a pass
to the in-coming striker. Who scores.

Commando

We lobbed grenades then charged,
shooting from the hip. I wanted
a Sten-gun or Schmeisser
but made do with a broken stick.

Girls weren't on the radar –
they did hopscotch, skipping,
couldn't whistle or throw for toffee –

until I saw Ann Sefton
twirling alone on a swing,
red face looking down,
and knew I didn't know what to say.

Bond

I scoured the atlas for Nassau,
stole a bow-tie from my father's drawer.
In code, listed the bullies at school –
then bumped them off one by one
with a silencer made from toilet roll tubes.

I wanted to be you.

That dark look, the chiselled jaw.
Fluent in French, a natural at skiing.
Adept at roulette, the quick-step;
seducer of beautiful women.

Only you could get away
with smoothing, *Well, hello Puss,*
or jaunt into the control room
to defuse a nuclear bomb, commenting on
the best way to serve a Dom Perignon.

One day I'd breeze through
the lab with Q, use a magnetic watch
to unzip the dress of a swooning girl.

Or just have a quip ready for Gary Murray
as he pasted my face into the playground wall.

The Myths of Greece and Rome

A green hard-back, text Times Roman
of course. A present from my mother,
on holiday in Crete, aged twelve:

olives at the taverna, piercing sun,
and a girl called Joanna who could have
launched a thousand ships one by one.

All week I fought Titans, fauns, put out
the flame-thrower of a chimera to win
her hand – not seeing how those kings

packed their daughters' suitors off
to slaughter, even less that my mother
might have given the book to warn me.

Netherland

I. 1980

I know *Love Will Tear Us Apart* is the best single ever
but not what its title means

I know that Sarah Hartley walks past me every Tuesday at four
but not that wearing Brut isn't cool

I know *The Life of Lord Byron* is better than his poems
but not if love is the same as it is in films

I know I've been picked for the Under-16s tour of Holland
but not that I'll puke five times into the North Sea

I know I'd rather go to the Dales without my parents
but not that I'll soon find Amsterdam the greatest place in the world

II. Laughing Cavalier

Mr Vliet drove us straight to a bar
after I'd scored my first fifty.
I'd been sea-sick the day before,
seen Amsterdam on a *rondvaart* –
his wife teasing how I was already
back on the water. He bought
Oranjeboom, Genevas, told a story
about an umpire from Yorkshire,
begging us not to be so boring.
I showed how I raised my bat
before Ian said the opposition
were only twelve year olds.
That's it, that's all I remember.
Just Mr V, Piet, Jan, Ian and me,
falling about, laughing, drinking.
And not being sick.

III. Place-names

Maasluis. Sloeterdijk.
The rush of water from
sluice gates to the sea.

Bloemendaal. Tulp.
Red and white quilts
of bulb fields in Spring.

Apeldoorn. Gouda.
Pale cheese in broodjes,
cows grazing orchards.

Landsmeer. Zeeland.
People heeling-in dykes
below that heavy sky.

IV. Night boat

Nothing happened, though
something was happening to me,
as that wake cut the stillness
below the moon, a film of cloud
over the sky's pewter blue.

I sat in a deckchair, alone,
neither lonely or cold,
looking back, the neat trees
and fields of Holland
a pencil line above the sea,

clear as the week before –
my first smoke, Mrs V's laugh
at her husband's jokes,
her worry I'd be sick, my face red
thinking she was so pretty.

And I am there now,
with that same disbelief
a night could be this light,
the North Sea so calm,
and already wanting to go back.

II. Holland

Things you learn at UEA

How to tell Roman from Romanesque,
Romantic from Neoclassical.
That women *go mad for it* after dinner.

That it was not the artist *per se* but patronage
which determined artistic production.
How to ensure bed was warm in winter.

That views on what comprised art
were largely set by the second century.
To avoid a job frying burgers at the Wimpy.

How much we owe to the word *landschapp*.
Not to blame bad grades on your tutor.
That it all happens in the last hour at Ritzy's.

That Turner strove for a striking effect.
How to use the pace and spin of the ball.
That keeping clothes in an old fridge was cool.

That Constable wanted only the truth.
How you have to master the material.
That life, like art, was entirely up to you.

Girls by Vermeer

read a letter by an open window
pour milk from a jug beside a wall

sew lace in a room with pale light
sit waiting by a map of the world

stand behind a lady writing a note
look at the chessboard tiled floor

smile with eyes bright as a pearl

Kathelijne

It is summer, and I see you for the first time –
pretending to march but getting it wrong,
immediately laughing with friends.

A week later too: wagging your finger
at a boy barely younger than you; showing
your group how to bat but forgetting to run.

You looked like the young Doris Day –
bright eyes, messy hair, always pleased
to see me with that whip-crack-away smile.

And like the first time, that thought
out of nowhere: that if I ever had a daughter,
I'd want her to be just the same as you.

Schipol

All flights lead here now,
to the bare meeting point
where I never met Kathy,
but waited another hour,
just in case, still hoping
to catch her smile, at least
seeing at last how it was
the same as my mother's.

Diary of a Young Girl

We can't ever look out the window.
                              Anne Frank

The inescapable truth is that
we know the end before the start.
Hard then not to think of the day
those quarrels stopped – how
Anne was learning dance steps
perhaps, or pausing to describe
the morning sky as lead or iron
when those boots clomped up
the stairs and the bookcase slid
back that final time to reveal
men for whom there could be
only one account, one outcome,
and never any shades of grey.

Green

Slices of kiwi fruit,
ash tree leaves;
broccoli and stilton soup,
the sofa my sister gave me.

Kryptonite,
jealousy;
Robin Hood in tights,
Beethoven's Pastoral Symphony.

Foothills,
Blackpool trams,
the paint-scheme in the bathroom;
Constable's Flatford Mill,
and the notepad in your hand
the first time I saw you.

Sventje

I. I remember

the sky, that blue silk
only winter mornings can produce,

and you waiting for
an endless line of cars to pass,

looking as beautiful as Mary Ure
in *Where Eagles Dare*.

I felt sick, cold inside,
unable to go through with it.

Excuse me. Do you have
the notes from that lecture?

Your friends looked on
like cattle peering at a stranger.

Oh that. No, it was the wrong one.
You see we are from Holland.

Then that faint smile.
Faint, that is, yet strong enough

to let a thousand doves stream
into the light-filled air.

II. On the way back

I was happy and sad and lost.
I was the street-lit fog around me,
the molecules of air dissolving
the Chemistry block into the dark.

And you were still there,
breath ghosting into mine,
that glint in your eyes
as we almost kissed good-bye.

Impossible really, to take it in:
how that morning we'd never met,
but for once I'd found
the mad guts to have a go –

to speak to you, I mean –
had even made your friends laugh
in The Champion of the Thames
then walked you back alone.

You would never write or call,
but deep-down I knew
I couldn't have done anything more
or better.

III. Thinking of you

I sloped off to open the parcel
with your refusal to the dance –
only to find a tulip, that single
by Sister Sledge, the word YES.
Then that compressed guitar,
the tune so happy and simple
it is a laughing boy running
under a sprinkler in summer,
my mother's garden perhaps –
daffodils trumpeting the news
from east to west, oak on bass,
sun-dial recording the hour,
and all the flowers swaying
in time with the chorus girls
as the world came into colour.

IV. At the river

we lay holding hands, gazing
at the sky through a tangled oak.
I was thinking we must look
like a starfish to the birds above,
and that this was happiness,
when you jolted to blurt out:
I shouldn't tell you, but last week
my brother tried to kill himself;
there was a family meal, then...

I sat up open-mouthed, held
you close, tears cool against
my sun-burnt neck, thinking
whatever must have happened
to him could happen to you.
Then nothing. Birdsong.
The drone of the distant A1.
Sunlight still drenching
that green expanse of fields.

V. Just before midnight

a rocket ripped
through the dark to fountain
into a palm tree, showering
cinders down slow as falling glitter.

I touched your hand in disbelief,
the words banging through me:
It's funny, but someone told me
dance partners often marry –

your smile lit up
by a boom bursting into bloom,
as if the night had raised a wand
to present the sky with flowers.

VI. The first time

I noticed
moonlight looks like frost
was that night in June
you looked out
over the slate rooftops
turning blue,
each one a lunar panel
taking in
the steady stream of white
and glistening
with frozen stars.

VII. The afternoon before you flew back

we cycled across Midsummer Common
then took a boat
through the unfenced fields,
the grey-green willows
of Grantchester Meadows.

You sat taking in
the swallows skimming
winking pools, their turns
like boomerang spins
about the reeds and shallows.

Nobody came or went,
except a dragonfly.
It lighted on the side,
body a bamboo tail pinned
with biplane wings and goggled eyes.

Neither of us moved
as it rested to refuel –
with light or food, we couldn't tell –
glowing coral to tinsel green,
purring through the colours of a rainbow.

It only stayed a minute or two,
then set off in a muslin whir,
a blue flame ghosting across the water –
into the light
and the rest of summer.

VIII. 7am, Wednesday 26th July

and I'm on the train from Vlissingen to Ede
where you are still sleeping.

Outside, mud-flats, sea grass, gulls;
a slender chimney feeding the sky with clouds.

Zeeland: polders, cows; a distant mist
below some pylons you might liken
to the masts of a grounded ship.

Low sun, flitting in endless glasshouse panes
to keep up with the train, as you stir,
thinking I'm still in England.

Mad, this, coming to your parents' a day early,
but your surprise will be worth it.

Zuid Holland, with cricket-flat fields,
turbines churning a breeze to Gouda.

Rotterdam; statues of commuters,
and an announcement for Tulp, which reminds
me to buy flowers for you and your mother.

IX. That night

we were in your room: you in bed,
me still dressed, saying I'd never been
to Delft, and how I liked your father –
his weary views, the way he gave
me thirty guilders with that nod –
Here, take it, take her out voor a meal –
words you never thought you'd hear,
face red, and breaking into tears.

X. You were out that Friday in September

when your mother told me it had to end,
then broke down crying, *It is so sad,*
so sad – you and she are so in love!

I didn't understand, or know what to do –
stepped forward to hug her,
but she drew back as if I was a mugger.

Perhaps I should answer those questions –
why do you like my daughter so much,
so you think you can buy her, do you –

hardly thinking accounts might differ,
with you more likely to believe
a strange relative than a relative stranger.

XI. No fizz or sparkle for you now

propped up with pillows,
coming round
to the darkness outside,
squeals of children
at the falling guy,
rocket pops and booms
dull thuds in an empty ward,
some starburst glitter
a pale red flicker
on its bare walls,
and still in the corner,
that overnight case
with the skirt and shoes
for the interview you made up
rather than tell your father.

XII. A train from Schipol, a cold walk to Ede

I had to know why it was over.

Your father wasted no time, shouting:
You had a fixed idea of things –
no interest in her independence, career!

You sat red-faced, looking at the TV –
an inside story on the Stasi,
its training methods and propaganda,

Berliners hammering down the Wall.

XIII. Leaving Ede

the father changed gear then stated:
You don't know Sventje. She is ambitious.
I sensed a nod but felt too flat to look,
staring ahead like a test crash dummy.
The car shot on, dashboard flashing
sepia-grey from the streetlights above
as if the present was already turning
into the past – all those cycle rides,
places we made love, the day you said
your Law degree was just for him –
while he confided: *I don't believe in
this one-and-only business. It is nonsense.*

XIV. The father

escorted me to the train like an armed guard. I put
my rucsac on a seat then returned to shake hands
like a good captain after cricket, maybe discuss
his next trip abroad,
                          but he'd gone, having slipped
down the underpass like a clever rat. His exit hit
me hard: he'd almost been the father I never had,
but to him I was history, a dead bird in the dirt.
What did he care if I got on or fell underneath?
All that mattered to him was I was out of the way,
and never coming back.

XV. I stood on the edge

the brown Amstel slapping the side below,
December sky blue as the day we met.
Your silence there from the night before,
his shouts too, my mother's words even
the previous week: *You do know I'd take*
the pain away if I could, don't you dear?
And everything undone: hopes, plans,
things to make you laugh – all washed out
by what was to come: the jump as I was,
mouth opening as if being sick in reverse,
hauled out days later by the city police –
news he'd milk for all it was worth,
making me see whatever he made out
I did, I could never do this to my mother.

View of Delft

We walk hand in hand by the Koornmarkt,
clacking over cobbles, too late again
for a rondvaart or the Prinsenhof museum.

Over low rooftops, glockenspiel bells clink
a slow version of Scarborough Fair.

Old houses with slender windows cram
the canal like moored schooner sterns.

The sun throws its last at the pink and blue.

The music box stops. I turn with a smile,
but you're not there anymore.

What I can't forget

is that week in the Dales:
how you went bright red

on signing the B&B book
in case we'd be discovered.

Then later, in the bath
as I shaved by the window

with its view of the valley:
stone walls, barns, trees

all stretched in shadow,
a mist like steam off cattle

and those low shafts of sun
I so wanted you to see.

Ravens over cornfields

after van Gogh

No morning sunlight here,
no almond blossom
in white and pink like
snowflakes out of the blue.
Just the dark of a storm,
this swarm of black wings
over the standing corn;
and that dirt track through
its centre, leading nowhere.

Girl writing a letter

Out of the blue, a letter from Kathy:
still at Leiden, doing law
with hockey, tennis, rowing and *rijding* –
living in a student house
with thirty girls – *all bitches of course!*

No *excuus* for not writing, but in love
with a boy with big ears; planning
to solve her debt *crijsis*
with another day at the races.
Thats too bad about that girl,
her family with so many *problemms,*
but hopefully I was still tall and *atheltic.*

I could see her doing it in one go,
in a bar or lecture, unconcerned
with spelling and grammar.
And that in the steeplechase of life,
I'd backed the wrong horse entirely.

The garden in autumn

Mist. Heavy, still.

Pale yellow dots the grey

with a leaf about to fall.

The Massacre of the Innocents

after Bruegel

But for the soldier dragging a child
from a house and the man kneeling
by the captain's horse, arms out
to beg for his infant son's life,
it could be a Christmas card scene –
village church and roofs all white,
figures grouped in a frozen space
as if to skate or fish through ice.

Which makes me wonder if Bruegel
thought Judea like Breda in winter,
only to notice those bare trees –
branches no more than black veins
in a lifeless sky – and how bright
the blood on trampled snow.

New Year's Eve

I was staring at the dark in Liz's lounge,
the fire burnt out, saliva down my chin,
trying to remember the last time I'd moved.

Could recall her leaving: snow had swirled
outside, printing little stars on every window.
But that was all. A whole day gone:
I might have killed someone and not known it.

By the chair, her list of things for me to do:
make bed; feed cat; watch Morse; CALL MUM.

Then like that, it all came back:
Ede, Delft, the argument with your mother.
And that you already had someone new.

III. Waterland

Return to Ede

I haven't been back for seventeen years,
but can see your mother at the table –
bouffant hair, face powdered white,
bone china set before me – the pause
as she slid into that high-backed chair
to burst the silence with those words:
Do not plan your life around my daughter.
You think you know her, but you don't.

The trees near Veenendaal

I'm sitting back in the garden at dusk,
low sunlight giving way to blue,
like that time we cycled through

cornfields, you in a floral dress,
shadows long ahead. I weaved
round yours, you sang *Eternal Flame*.

The next day we made love
in a wood of young ash, oak; stayed
there all afternoon. I remember

the way we lay, the leaves
already brown, how they sifted
with the breeze. And now I wonder

if you ever went back – to listen
to the trees in evening light, or sit
and think how much they've grown.

Was it you

I saw at the lights in Den Haag,
hair still long, face changed to red
and looking as shocked as me
in the window of a battered Ford;
not what I'd have expected
given that all-important career
your father used to stress,
which made me wonder
if things hadn't worked out,
or if you ever recalled the day
we met at a crossing
then talked late into the night
without mentioning jobs at all.

Zuid Holland

The morning train is passing
a Mondrian of moated fields.

No birds or clouds drift by,
the horizon holds back the sea.

Prison-bar shadows slant
to some poplars and cyclists

that could be you and me,
and the child we never had.

Polder

It is always there,
that afternoon by the Rijn,

you in my sweater, relating
your father's views on careers,

explaining the word *polder* –
the dyke a man-made wall

over which to pump water out
and stop it flooding back –

how well-planned, managed;
how subtly controlled.

Exile in Utrecht

I'm lost in the king-size bed of this room:
blank walls, curtains drawn, the silence
filled with his shouts twenty years after
I last saw you. A down-light darkens
my Hancock face in the glass as I see
yours the day we cycled to Rhenen –
and still picture that return to expose
his lies and right the wrongs of the past.

Lowland

I. Et in Arcadia ego

You know the scene: open fields, feather trees,
and, in the foreground, a shepherdess singing
the latest Mozart tune to reclining friends
who must think life a picnic, but fail to see

that figure lurking to the left – a skeleton
with hourglass and scythe, mouth open-wide
as if already having the last laugh.

A bit like Sventje's father, I suppose, driving
from the station that night – me packed off
elsewhere and she duped into thinking
I wanted her just for sex – his hollow laugh

like an arcade machine nobody can switch off,
laughing and laughing and laughing
until the day she died.

II. Funerals

I knew there'd be the odd one now and then,
old timers mostly, people I didn't really know –
my father's golf partners and drinking cronies,
the lady who made jam from over the road.

But nearing fifty, the mortgage and parents gone,
it seems more and more that a crash or cancer
chalks up another one, and I'm back in black,
part-funding some church I'll never see again.

I've even bought a suit. It hangs in a wardrobe
in the spare room – out of sight but there,
quietly waiting for some family's red-raw stares,
faces frozen with the dawn that never comes.

I know life ends with death, that it doesn't go
on like an atomic clock. Only it feels that
some time soon it'll be me packed up
by the bus stop, *just waiting in the next room.*

Which makes me wish, not for a full house,
light streaming in, white flowers everywhere,
but rather a dull service – maybe just the vicar
and undertaker – no one I knew even there.

III. Afterwards

I went back to the spot where we spent an afternoon –
the river a gleam in the dark, sky a braille of stars.

We watched a *kahn* lug coal to Koblenz or Köln,
a line of shirts in surrender from bridge to stern.

I lay with my head on Sventje's lap while she fed me
some apricot flan – but only if I said *sinaasappelsap*.

Things I sensed would return again and again,
like a guide light that booms out of the night

then stops, leaving the drizzled tail of its reflection
in the mind long after the light has gone.

IV. Landscape with no figures skating

February: the Herengracht green,
no reflections of trees.

A flurry of snow chalks gables
onto the houses by Leidsestraat.

No skaters below, scarfs flowing
like flags on a man-of-war,

or any children chasing a puck
towards the goal of some bridge.

Stranger still that Sventje took
me here on a rondvaart once –

and squeezed my hand then
raised her eyebrows after

pointing out the spot where
her father proposed to her mother.

V. The things she gave me

I still have the things she gave me,
hidden in a secret place.
Letters tell how we used to be,
photos let me touch her face.

Hidden in a secret place,
an old tape brings back the past.
Photos let me touch her face,
the poems she wrote let love last.

An old tape brings back the past.
Letters tell how we used to be.
The poems she wrote let love last.
I still have the things she gave me.

VI. Summer ghost

The sky is Delft blue,
the moon a brooch
in ivory and pearl.
It lights up trees,
roof-tops, turning
them all to stone.

Sventje sleeps,
a faint outline
on the bed like
a figure on a tomb.

From the corner,
Vini Reilly's guitar.
Requiem Again.

It is the only sound
in the room.

Outside,
there is no wind,

no movement.

Not even
        those hands

rise
        then
                fall

with

        her

                breathing.

I want

    to touch

        her,

see

  that smile

    take form,

but

  she

    has

already

    gone,

over

  the

    woods

  and

distant

    fields

Gelderland

To see the sun so high,
so late – solitary

in the beaten gold
of this August sky –

is to wonder how
it could ever sink

beyond the Rijn,
where poplars reflect

then give way to
a rower pulling back

towards the blue
of those woods

and a snow-capped
range of clouds.

Oostvaarderplassen

Redshank. Curlew. Snipe.
How the words present
colours, features, quirks.

Pipit. Warbler. Smew.
Their calls already there,
cries over the marsh at dawn.

Wagtail. Greylag. Tern.
The way they walk, take
flight into the clear blue air.

Walking with animals

I will now take a stroll by the broad canals of Leiden,
unsure if the town is flooding or sinking, but glad
to be crossing this bridge to the Botanical Gardens

with its hot-house of palms and flowers gathered
from every rainforest, savannah – the roof so high
a giraffe could graze the eucalyptus and bamboo.

I came here once with Sventje, after some lecture
from her father. We stood in its sapping heat,
amazed by a lily big enough to cover a hippo,

half-expecting to hear a parakeet screech or spot
a leopard dozing in a tree. And everywhere,
that Florida of colour: azaleas, orchids, evergreens

out of a children's giant picture book of the zoo.
She studied the Latin names of grasses and ferns,
explained the inter-dependency of species,

but I was for horsing around – hiding behind
a banana leaf, asking if that elephant house smell
meant she'd now found her ecological niche.

And we are still there, with tigers, zebra, bears –
not one snarling, no thoughts about the father –
all walking to that island above the rising water.

Reprise

I'd almost forgotten the morning
after our first night together

until I heard that piece again –
Mozart, I think, or maybe Chopin –

but definitely the one she played
sotto, slow, each note a tip-toe

up the stairs to the bath where
I lay watching the steam billow

towards the old sash window
as water plinked from the tap.

Somewhere in the distance

thunder is rolling boulders into super-quarry trucks
as summer rain pitters the windscreen, and I am back
to the night it drilled the roof of the grounded Mini,
Sventje aghast at my command to take off her shoe.
I disappeared outside once more, strafed by the storm,
to tie dangling exhaust to rusted bumper. Then back,
just praying it'd work, to pull away with a bump
and a scrape, before driving the next forty miles
in second gear, all hope of us reaching Diss hanging
on the shoelace holding up the arse of my sister's car.

Going out

A lemon scent in the crowd moves
in an unseen cloud, as if her hands were
about to clap over my eyes in that room –
white walls, single bed, notes buried
under bracelets, tissues, creams –
and that green box, black rings to the top –
Givenchy or Guerlain, I think, hopeless
with names – the perfume waiting
to be dabbed behind each ear,
head tilted back from that long hair
to show me the delicious curve of her neck.

Sventje sleeps

in the moonlight

her pale back lost
in drifts of sheets

where I want to
plant tiny kisses

    like

        a

    trail

        of

    little

        cat

    feet

        in

    the

        snow

Theo van Gogh

To read their letters now is to see
him at a gas-lit desk in the Rue Lepic,
canvasses of rooms and sunflowers unsold,
working out how much
to send on to his desperate brother.

No thought about those dirty clothes,
that disagreeable smell,
just this new crisis,
worse than all the others,
if the Infirmary at Saint-Remy was
the right place for one in his condition.

Which makes me think of Liz –
unable to answer those burning questions
on how and why Sventje left,
but writing out a list of things
for me to do, making sure
at least I had a square meal inside –

and how van Gogh must have staggered
from the cornfield that day,
clutching his chest,
less than thirty hours to live,
knowing some debts can never be repaid,
some things always left unsaid.

Vondelpark

I jog down a boulevard of trees towards
the Monet bridges my guidebook says
are worth the trip – an easy overtake
for the regulars in better shape and kit,
or on bikes borrowed from a Forties film.

How effortless they make it look, pushing
to work or a lover by the water's edge.
But then nothing here is too much trouble.

Except being one of them. I tried it once,
near Amstelveen. But people weren't
quite so laid-back as they seemed,
the cycle lanes not always lined with trees.

Maybe today the tramps will look up
from their papers, call me *kempenlander*,
friend – and to my amazement I'll reply
in my mother's mother tongue.

Instead, I plod on past a Tai Chi class,
some municipal gardeners in their truck,
that reed marsh with nesting storks.

I was always on the outside, looking on,
and I look on still, at the passers-by,
like figures from a dream –
lovers, lawyers, fathers –
and all the other things I could have been.

Thinking of Holland

I see broad rivers
drift through
endless plains
rows of poplars
like smoke plumes
far away

and throughout
that sunken space
woods farms fields
churches elms
both scattered
and as one

the sun is low
and sinks through
woven mists
towards the water
with its cries
from long ago

Notes

'1980': after *Love Will Tear Us Apart* by Joy Division, Factory Records, 1980.

'Thinking of you': after *Thinking Of You* by Sister Sledge, Cotillion Records, 1984.

'The trees near Veenendaal': after *Eternal Flame* by The Bangles, Columbia Records, 1989.

'Summer ghost': after *Requiem Again* by The Durutti Column, Factory Once, 1996.

'Thinking of Holland': after *Herinnering aan Holland* by Hendrik Marsman, 1936.